EDGE BOOKS™

Prepare to Survive

How to Survive a

Tornado

by Michael Martin

Consultant: Al Siebert, PhD
Author of *The Survivor Personality*

Capstone
press®

Mankato, Minnesota

Edge Books are published by Capstone Press,
151 Good Counsel Drive, P.O. Box 669, Mankato, Minnesota 56002.
www.capstonepress.com

Library of Congress Cataloging-in-Publication Data
Martin, Michael, 1948–
How to survive a tornado / by Michael Martin.
p. cm. — (Edge books. Prepare to survive.)
Summary: "Briefly presents specific survival strategies that can be used in a
tornado" — Provided by publisher.
Includes bibliographical references and index.
ISBN-13: 978-1-4296-2278-3 (hardcover)
ISBN-10: 1-4296-2278-4 (hardcover)
1. Tornadoes — Juvenile literature. 2. Emergency management — Juvenile
literature. I. Title.
QC955.2.M37 2009
613.6'9 — dc22   2008030750

Editorial Credits
Carrie A. Braulick, editor; Veronica Bianchini, designer; Wanda Winch,
    photo researcher; Sarah Schuette, photo stylist; Marcy Morin,
    photo shoot scheduler

Photo Credits
Alamy/Roger Coulam, 27 (top); AP Images/Chad Love, 21; AP Images/J. Pat
Carter, 28; AP Images/News-Courier/Alissa Clark, 16; AP Images/Tom Gannam,
25; Capstone Press/Karon Dubke, 8 (helmet), 10 (siren), 11, 12, 14, 17 (both), 18
(both), 19, 20, 22, 26, 29; ©1991 Gene E. Moore, 15; Corbis/Eric Nguyen, 4–5;
DigitalVision, 10 (background); FEMA News Photo/Adam Dubrowa, 9; FEMA
News Photo/Greg Henshall, 13 (both); FEMA News Photo/Michael Raphael, 6;
Getty Images Inc./The Image Bank/ A. T. Willett, 8 (tornado); Getty Images Inc./
Melanie Blanding, 27 (bottom); Getty Images Inc./Stone/Alan R. Moller, cover;
Rod Whigham, 23, 24; Shutterstock/Lora Liu, backcover (grunge notebook)

1 2 3 4 5 6 14 13 12 11 10 09

Table of Contents

Chapter 1

In a Tornado's Path

4

meteorologist – a person who studies and predicts the weather
funnel cloud – a funnel-shaped cloud that comes down from the
base of a thundercloud

It's a warm summer day. In the late afternoon, you notice towering storm clouds off to the southwest. At first, you don't think much about it. Then the sky grows darker. The wind begins to blow. You turn on the TV and hear a **meteorologist** giving a report. He says that conditions are right for tornadoes to form.

Just then, it starts to rain hard. When you look out your window, you notice something strange. Beneath a dark cloud hangs what looks like a rope or an elephant's trunk. It lowers to the ground and begins stirring up dust. As it passes over a house, you are horrified to see the roof lift off and blow away.

Suddenly, you realize that you're watching a tornado! The twisting, ropelike thing you see is the tornado's **funnel cloud**. And it's headed straight for your house!

You probably only have a few moments to decide how to protect yourself. What will you do?

TORNADO DANGERS

Few things on this planet are as terrifying as a tornado. Wind speeds inside these storms can top 300 miles (483 kilometers) per hour. When tornadoes touch the ground, the results can be horrible. The strongest tornadoes destroy nearly everything in their paths. Cars, trees, and even people can be picked up and thrown hundreds of yards. Tornadoes can completely flatten neighborhoods and small towns. They have killed more than 10,000 people in the United States since 1900.

TORNADOES EVERYWHERE

Tornadoes have been reported all over the world, but more occur in the United States than anywhere else. Tornadoes have hit every state. They can strike during any season, but tornadoes are most common in spring and summer.

Most U.S. tornadoes form in the middle of the country. In fact, so many roar through Kansas, Oklahoma, and other nearby states that the area is called Tornado Alley.

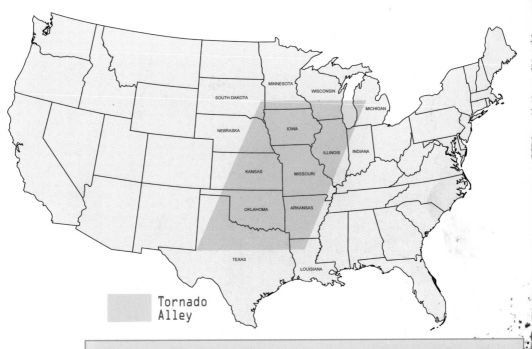

Tornado Alley

Scientists do not agree on the exact location of Tornado Alley. This Tornado Alley map is based on the number of tornadoes per 1,000 square miles (2,590 square kilometers).

FLYING OBJECTS

People often think the greatest danger of a tornado is being lifted into the air. That can happen, but it is rare. Most victims die after being struck in the head by flying objects. A flying piece of wood or glass can be as deadly as a bullet.

TIP: You can use a bicycle or skateboarding helmet to protect your head during a tornado.

CRUMBLING BUILDINGS

People also die when buildings collapse during tornadoes. Some people are crushed by falling roofs or walls. Others die when furniture or other heavy objects fall on them.

Some people become trapped inside collapsed buildings. These people could suffer from **dehydration**. Trapped people who are severely injured can die if they don't get to a hospital in time.

dehydration – a medical condition caused by a lack of water

Chapter 2

How to Survive

TIP: Be especially watchful of tornadoes between 2:00 in the afternoon and 6:00 in the evening. About 40 percent of tornadoes in the United States strike between these times.

Would you know what to do if you were in a tornado's path? Keep reading to be sure the decisions you make are wise ones.

STAY AWARE!

People who stay aware are least likely to die in a tornado. If rainstorms or thunderstorms are in the area, listen to the radio or watch TV every few minutes. If conditions are right for a tornado to form, meteorologists will issue a tornado watch for your area. This means tornadoes are possible in your area.

If a tornado is sighted, meteorologists will issue a tornado warning. Often, they will announce the tornado's direction and speed. The warning gives people in the tornado's path time to take cover.

Some towns have sirens that are sounded after a warning is issued. But there is not always enough time to sound a siren before a tornado hits. Never assume you're safe because you haven't heard a siren.

IF YOUR HOME HAS A BASEMENT

If your home has a basement, consider yourself lucky. A basement is often the best place to take cover from a tornado. If you have a cell phone, grab it before heading downstairs. A cell phone could be useful if you are trapped under **debris**.

An interior room without windows is the safest place in a basement. Strong winds can shatter glass into hundreds of sharp, deadly pieces.

If possible, crawl under a heavy workbench or other sturdy piece of furniture. These items can offer protection if the walls collapse or the roof caves in. Otherwise, crouch down and try to protect your head with your arms.

Another safe place is under the stairway. The stairs can keep heavy objects from falling on you.

debris — the scattered pieces of something that has been broken or destroyed

JUST IN TIME!

On May 4, 2007, Laura Prosser and her two children were at home in Greensburg, Kansas. Laura knew that severe thunderstorms were in the area. When the tornado siren sounded, she knew exactly what to do. She and her children rushed to the basement. They huddled together in a corner. Soon, the electricity failed and the lights went out. The family members heard glass breaking all around them.

After the noise stopped, they saw destruction everywhere. The tornado had destroyed their home, as well as nearly all the other homes in Greensburg. The tornado killed 11 people.

Damage from the tornado that hit Greensburg, Kansas, in May 2007

TIP: Before you take cover in your basement, consider where heavy furniture is located on the main level of the house. Don't take cover directly under these objects.

What if

YOU DON'T HAVE A BASEMENT?

Many homes in southern states don't have basements. If your house lacks a basement, take cover in a room on the lowest floor of your house. Stay away from windows. If the room has a table, crawl under it for extra protection.

An interior bathroom is one of the best places to take shelter. Close the door and climb into the bathtub. The bathtub is often the only thing not blown away when a tornado destroys a house. If you have time, grab a blanket and wrap it around yourself. You can also grab a mattress and pull it over your body. A pillow will provide extra protection for your head. If you don't have time to grab anything, wrap your arms around your head.

SAVED BY THE BATHTUB

On April 26, 1991, at least 54 tornadoes struck the southern United States. The storms killed 24 people. Many others had narrow escapes. Near Wichita, Kansas, a man climbed into his bathtub just before a powerful tornado hit. As the man's house broke apart, the pipes

holding the bathtub snapped. The tub spun around the room like a ride at an amusement park. Then it shot out the front door with the man still inside. Although the tub flipped over and trapped him underneath, it also kept him from being seriously hurt.

TIP: Wind speeds inside a tornado increase with height. No matter where you are when a tornado threatens, get as low as possible.

What if

YOU'RE IN A MOBILE HOME?

If you're in a mobile home during a tornado warning, your survival instructions are simple. Get out! Tornadoes often send mobile homes tumbling through the air. If your mobile home park has a tornado shelter, go there. If not, go to a nearby building. Take cover in an interior room on the lowest floor. Any other building is better than being in a mobile home.

Tornado shelters are often made of concrete.

TIP: Grab your shoes before taking shelter from a tornado. The shoes will protect your feet if a tornado scatters debris everywhere.

What if

YOU'RE AT SCHOOL?

What if you hear a tornado siren while waiting for a ride home from basketball practice? Most schools have places assigned as tornado shelters. If your school doesn't, go to a hallway in the middle of the school on the lowest floor. Stay far away from doors and windows. Avoid gymnasiums or auditoriums. Their roofs can be ripped away in a tornado.

TORNADO
SHELTER

IF YOU'RE IN A SHOPPING MALL?

Shopping malls are dangerous during a tornado because most storefronts are made of glass. A hallway without windows or a small storage room is a good place to take shelter. A bathroom without windows is another. Stay away from large open areas where a roof could easily collapse.

Stay away from glass storefronts if you're in a mall during a tornado warning.

19

What if

YOU'RE IN A CAR?

Think you can outrun a tornado in a car? Think again. The direction and speed of a tornado are hard to predict. Some tornadoes have even traveled in circles! You might think a car provides good protection in a tornado. After all, you are surrounded by more than 2,000 pounds (900 kilograms) of sturdy metal. But tornadoes can easily toss cars into the air.

Tell the driver to stop if you're in a car during a tornado warning. Then get out. Seek shelter inside a nearby building on the lowest floor.

If there are no buildings nearby, lay down flat in the lowest spot you can find. A ditch or a **culvert** could work well. Wrap your arms around your head and neck to protect yourself from flying debris. Do not take cover under an overpass. Debris is often blown under an overpass in a tornado. You can also easily be sucked out from under an overpass.

culvert — a water drain; culverts often cross under roads or sidewalks.

What if

A TORNADO STRIKES AT NIGHT?

Tornadoes that occur at night are deadlier because they can't be seen. That is why it's so important to listen to the radio or TV for warnings. If you live in an area where tornadoes strike often, you should have a weather radio. These radios sound an alarm if a tornado warning is announced. The loud noise should wake you even if you are sound asleep.

TIP: Hold your shirt over your mouth and nose if dust is in the air after a building collapse.

What if

YOU'RE TRAPPED?

What if your "safe" location wasn't so safe after all and you're trapped under debris? First, stay calm. Don't shout for help unless you know rescue workers are nearby. Yelling will only tire you. Stay as still as possible to save your energy.

If you have them, use a whistle or a cell phone to call for help. You can also pick up two sturdy objects and knock them together to make a tapping noise. Tap three times, pause, and tap three times again. Rescue workers will be listening for this pattern.

YOU'RE CARRIED AWAY?

Tornadoes usually don't pick up people off the ground. But it can happen. If this happens to you, do everything possible to protect your head. Most people are knocked unconscious by flying debris. Keep your eyes closed to keep debris out of them.

The tornado will probably drop you on the ground before you can prepare to land. But if you can, bend your knees and relax before landing. Then roll as you hit the ground.

BLOWN AWAY!

Rick Boland and his son Craig were at their home near St. Mary, Missouri, on March 11, 2006. Shortly after 9:00 at night, Craig told his father that the sky looked funny. Just then, the wind howled and the house shook.

Rick and Craig ran to the bathroom. Craig climbed into the bathtub. Then the electricity failed. In the darkness, Rick and Craig waited. They heard a loud whooshing noise above them. Rick later said that it was the loudest noise he had ever heard. The house broke apart into pieces. Before they knew what was happening, Rick and Craig were lifted into the air. Rick kept his eyes closed. Flying objects slammed into Rick and Craig as they spun uncontrollably.

Then Rick and Craig fell hard to the ground. About 30 pieces of wood were stuck in Rick's body. Craig suffered broken bones, a punctured lung, and a cut to his ear. The tornado had carried Rick and Craig about 100 yards (91 meters).

NOT IN THE CLEAR YET

You may think the danger is over when a tornado has passed. That could be a big mistake. Tornadoes sometimes travel in groups. Keep listening to weather reports on the radio or TV.

Even if no more tornadoes are expected, there can be danger. Downed power lines or damaged electrical wires could shock you. Stay far away from these hazards.

Don't walk around in the dark after a tornado. Grab a flashlight to help you see. Tornado victims sometimes light candles to help them see in the dark. But this is a bad idea. Leaking gas lines from a gas stove or furnace can cause an explosion.

Other dangers are present after a tornado. Steer clear of glass, nails, and other debris. Stay far away from damaged buildings. They could still collapse.

TIP: If a tornado severely damages your home, use a wrench to shut off the gas supply to the house.

Some people build a safe room on the first floor of their house. These strengthened rooms provide extra protection during a tornado.

BE PREPARED, BUT NOT AFRAID

In recent years, tornado warning systems have improved. Since 2000, only about 50 people each year have died during tornadoes in the United States. Chances are good that you will never have to put your newly learned survival skills into practice. But if you do, your odds of living through a tornado are even greater.

TIP: Make an emergency meeting place with your family. If you become separated after a tornado or other disaster, you'll be able to find one another again.

BUILD A SURVIVAL KIT

Prepare for a tornado or other natural disaster by making a survival kit. Keep your kit in an area that is handy to all family members. Make sure everyone knows where the kit is located. Include these items:

- gas shut-off wrench
- bottled water
- canned or dried food
- nonelectric can opener
- first-aid kit, including any necessary prescription medications

- flashlight
- battery-operated radio
- cell phone or CB radio
- extra batteries
- clothing and bedding
- whistle

Glossary

culvert (KUHL-vurt) — a water drain; culverts often cross under a road or a sidewalk.

debris (duh-BREE) — the scattered pieces of something that has been broken or destroyed

dehydration (dee-hy-DRAY-shuhn) — a medical condition caused by a lack of water

funnel cloud (FUHN-uhl KLOUD) — a cone-shaped cloud that is usually a visible part of a tornado; a funnel cloud is wide at the top and narrow at the bottom.

meteorologist (mee-tee-ur-AWL-uh-jist) — a person who studies and predicts the weather

overpass (OH-vur-pass) — a road that crosses over and above another road

unconscious (uhn-KON-shuhss) — not awake or able to respond to others

Read More

Ceban, Bonnie J. *Tornadoes: Disaster and Survival.* Deadly Disasters. Berkeley Heights, N.J.: Enslow, 2005.

Jeffrey, Gary. *Tornadoes & Superstorms.* Graphic Natural Disasters. New York: Rosen, 2007.

Morris, Neil. *Inside Hurricanes and Tornadoes.* Inside Nature's Disasters. Milwaukee: Gareth Stevens, 2007.

Woods, Michael, and Mary B. Woods. *Tornadoes.* Disasters Up Close. Minneapolis: Lerner, 2007.

Internet Sites

FactHound offers a safe, fun way to find educator-approved Internet sites related to this book.

Here's what you do:

1. Visit *www.facthound.com*
2. Choose your grade level.
3. Begin your search.

This book's ID number is 9781429622783.

FactHound will fetch the best sites for you!

Index